BE AFRAID

then do it anyway

Published by Last Lemon Productions
60 Woodside Dr. San Anselmo,
CA 94960, USA

ISBN 978-1-7332675-5-7

First Printing, 2019

www.lastlemon.com

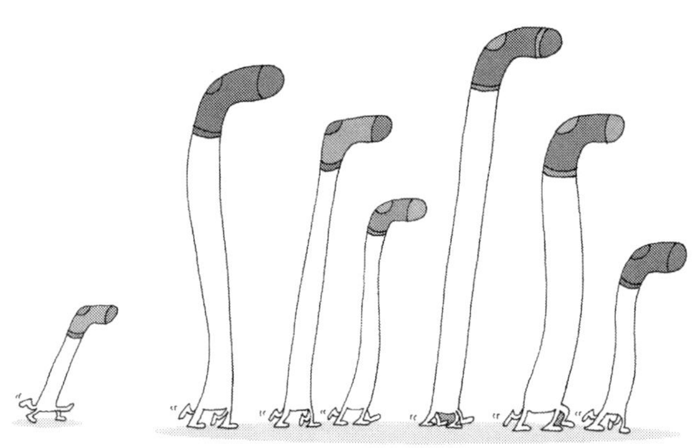

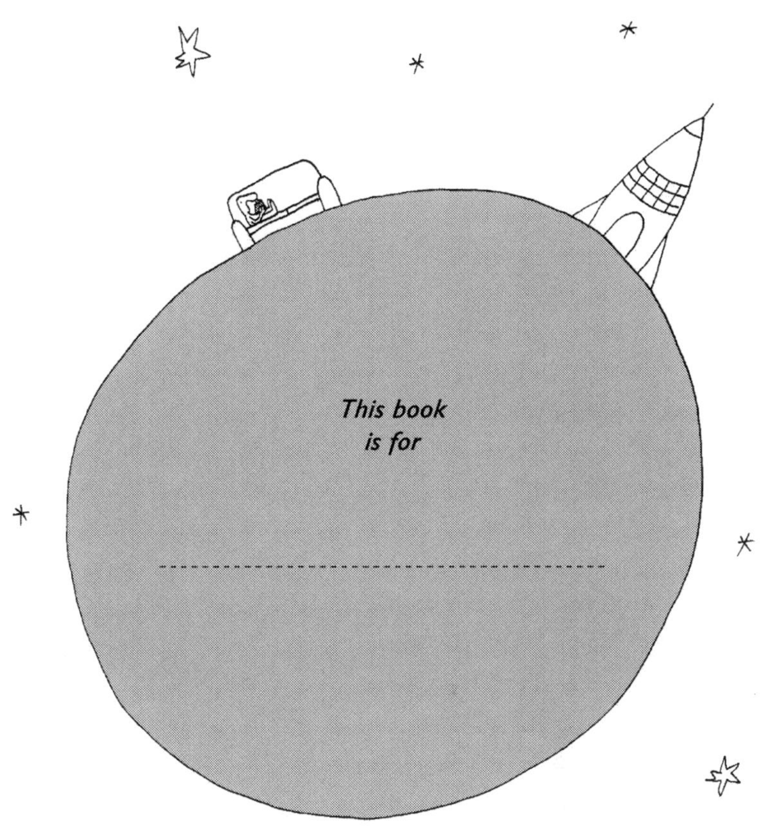
This book
is for

Hello,

If you've only just arrived, welcome to Harold's Planet!

Harold has been marching to the beat of his own drum for over twenty years now. Up mountains that scratch the clouds, through a sea of faces, via London, Paris, Cape Town, the Kalahari, Maui, Mexico and Northern California.

Whether enjoying the finer things in life (warm breezes, red wine, an open fire, head-scratching), exploring, inventing, being curious, defying convention, or simply contemplating the weirdness and beauty of life, he faces it all with his signature blend of indefatigable optimism, refreshing honesty and silliness.

Dare to be inspired by Harold, as we have, to do things your *own* way.

Lisa + Ralph

Lisa Swerling + Ralph Lazar

*"Life isn't about finding yourself.
Life is about creating yourself."*

George Bernard Shaw

Signs of Happiness

Some days are just quite octopusish...

Nothing quite like an open flame
and something nice to cook

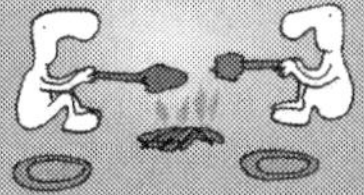

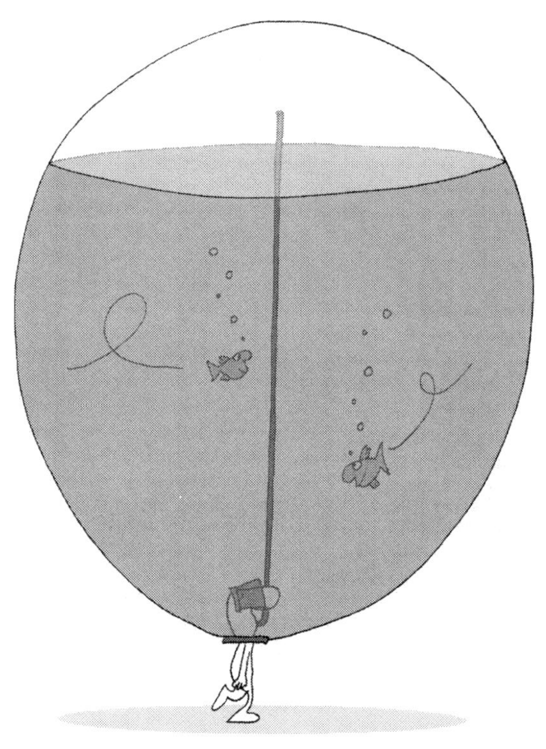

Bear with me, I'm having a beach-hole-kind-of-day

INSIDE-OUT T-SHIRT DAY

MAKING THE MOST OUT OF A MESSY SITUATION

The Perfect Certainty of Uncertainty

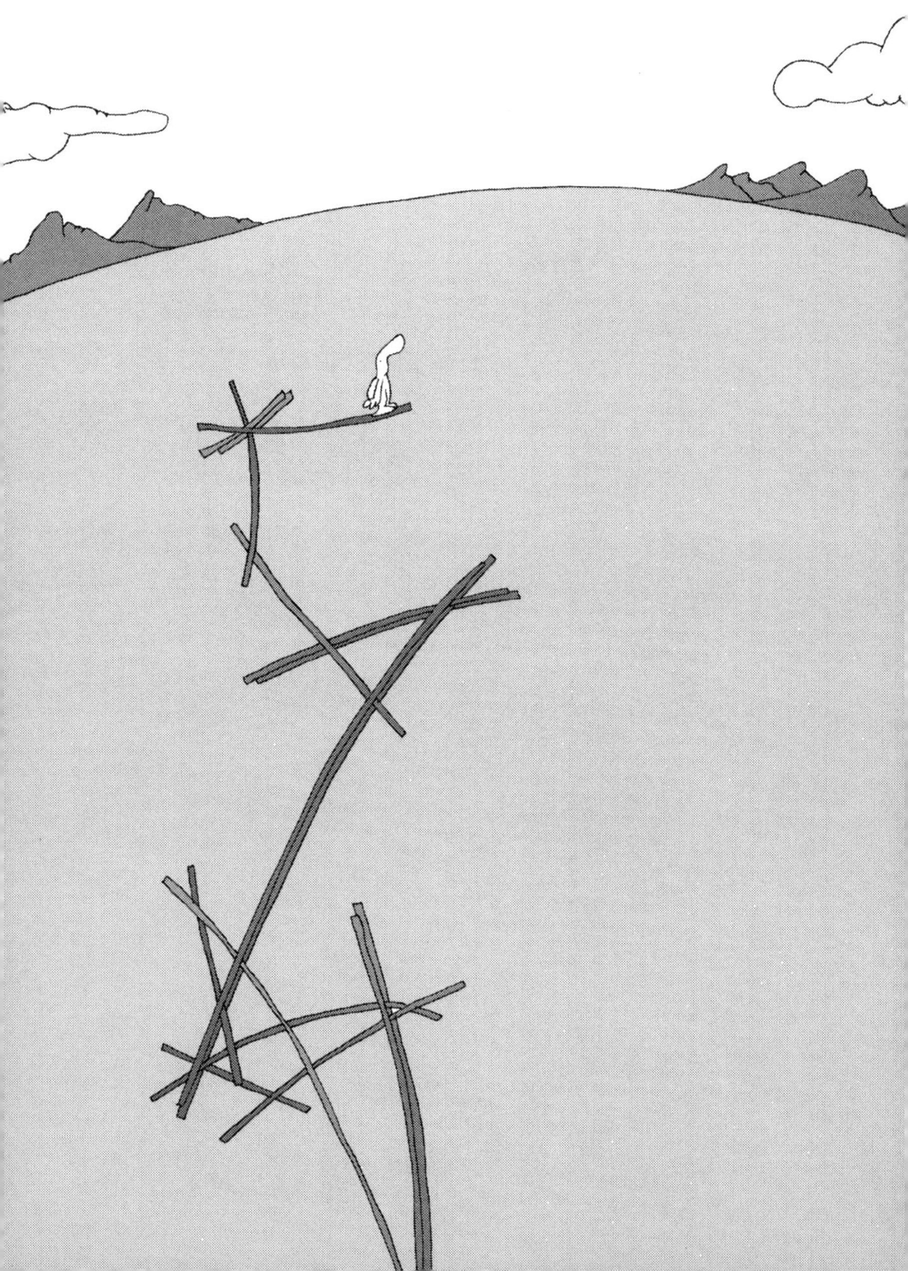

Always

take a tomato with you,

just in case...

Free-range toasters

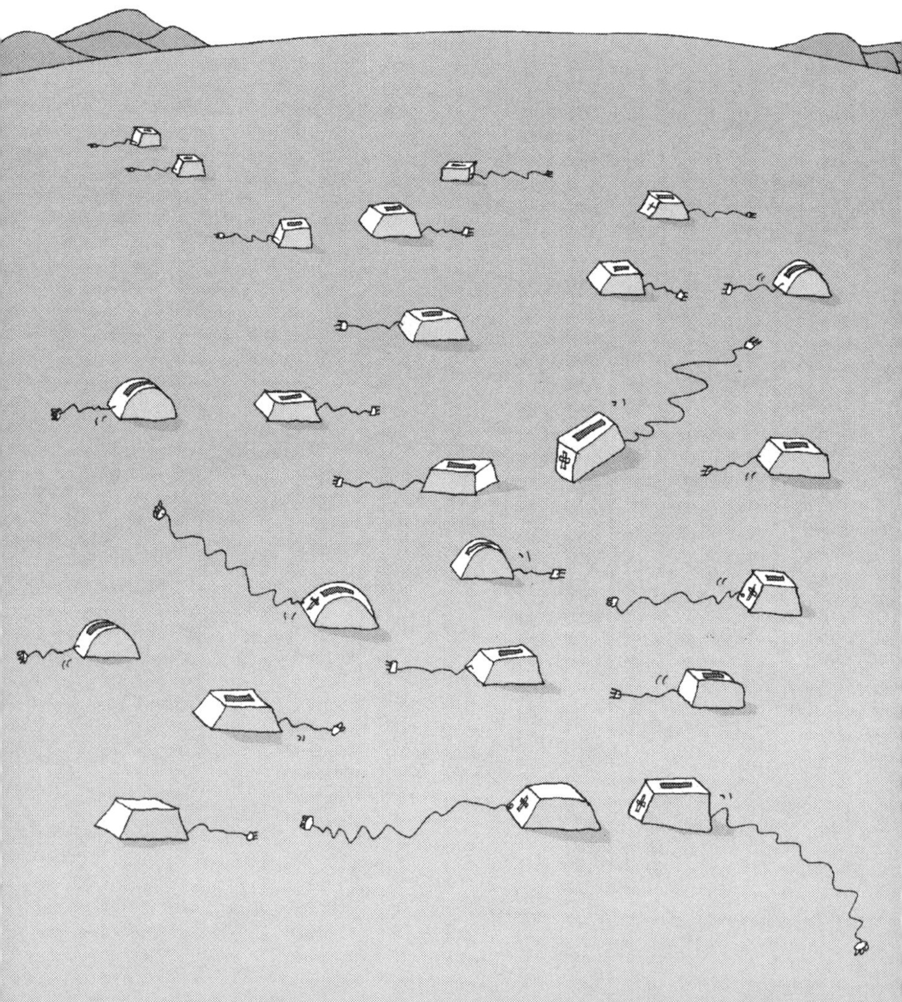

Some days you just have to embrace the weirdness

If in doubt,
always wave.

Addicted to books,
it's official

3 reasons to be CHEERFUL

[1] Because
[2] Garlic
[3] Exists

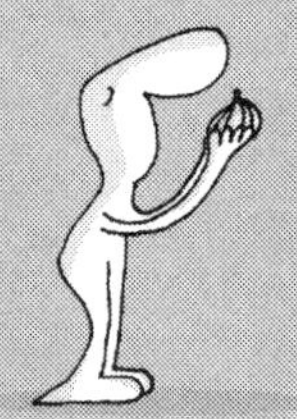

Corporate Ladders

Hammock (non-corporate)

I regret having had 8 hours sleep...

- said no-one, ever

THINK OUT
OF THE

Skinny-dipping in the moonlight

Poo
with a view

Why do I always carry
a little knife with me?
Well, it's in case one of those
delicious little French saucissons
comes trotting along
of course....

How to *Deal with Life*

NO

YES

Just in case...

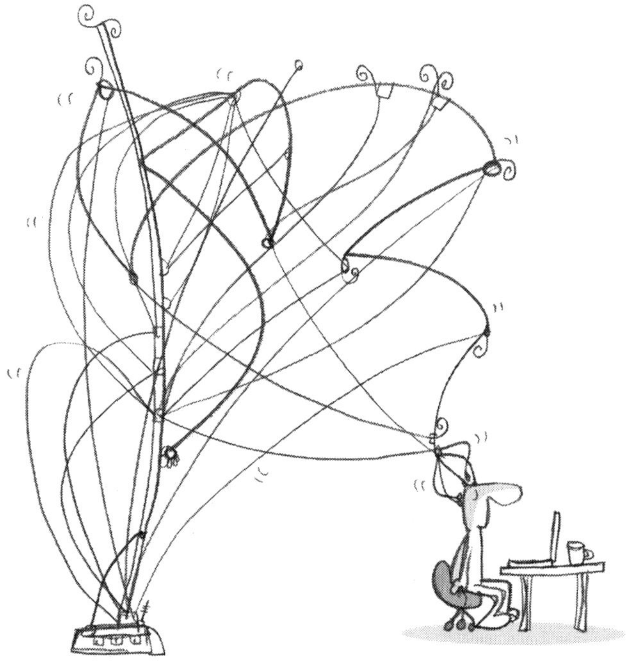

Dream Jobs #2

Quality Control: Head-scratching Devices

SIMPLE PLEASURES #12

The first cup of coffee

The Indefatigable Optimism of the Traveling Fridge Salesmen

Happiness is...

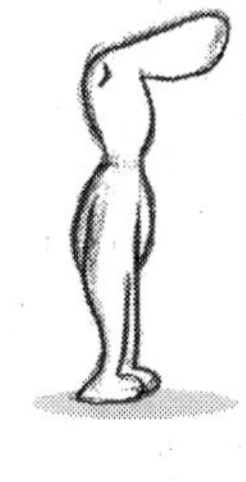

no network coverage

If in doubt,

stand up and paddle

Official Fieldguide to
HAROLD'S PLANET

The Mainly Smile

Happiness is...
the sound of rain on the window

Hiccups!

We are all
wonderfully
weirder
than we think
we are

HOW TO FACE THE FUTURE

1. Be nice to everyone.

2. Don't spend too much time talking about politics.

3. Make art

4. Spend more time in nature.

***Pet** De-stressers*

Cats

Dogs

Aardvarks

Grisbiums

The happy writer

9 months later...

Some call it greed.
I call it **joie de vivre.**

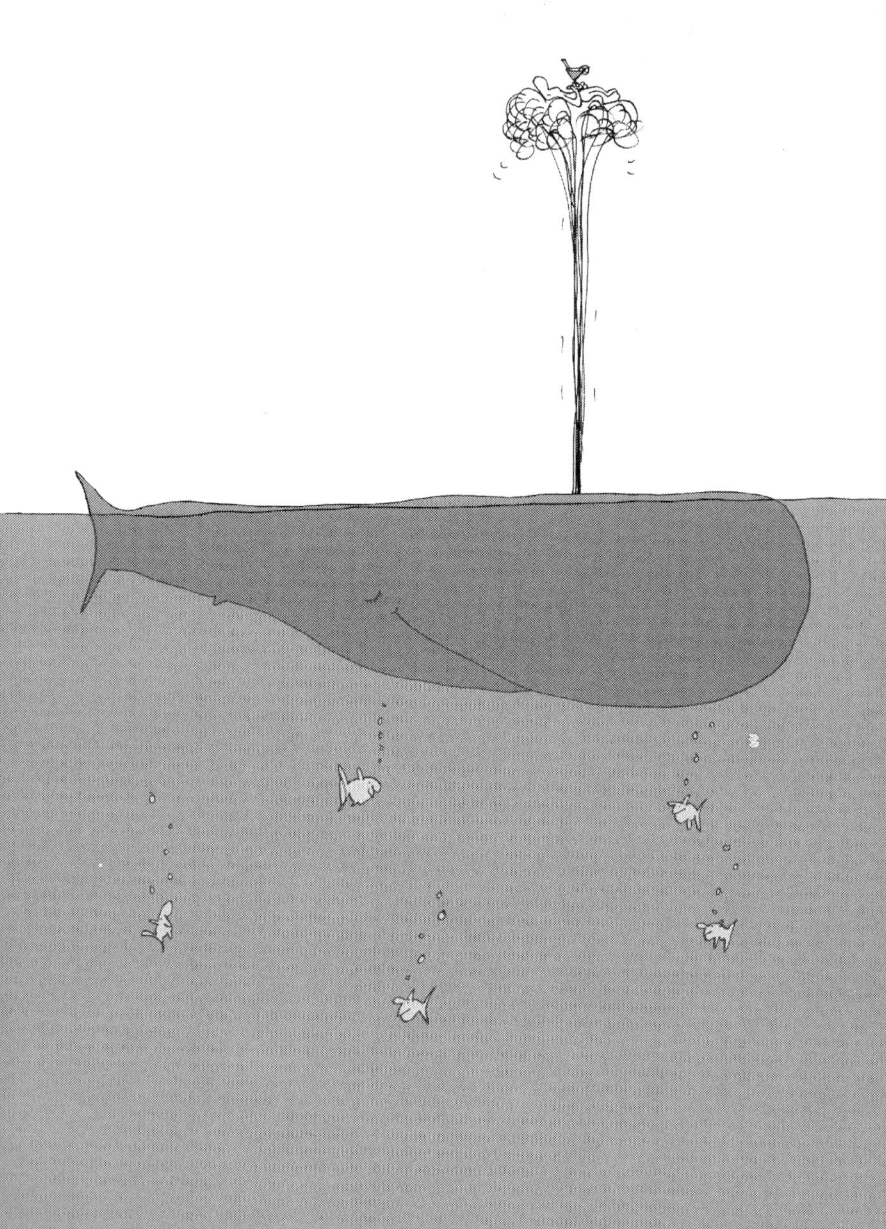

How to *Walk your Dog if you Live on a Small Planet*

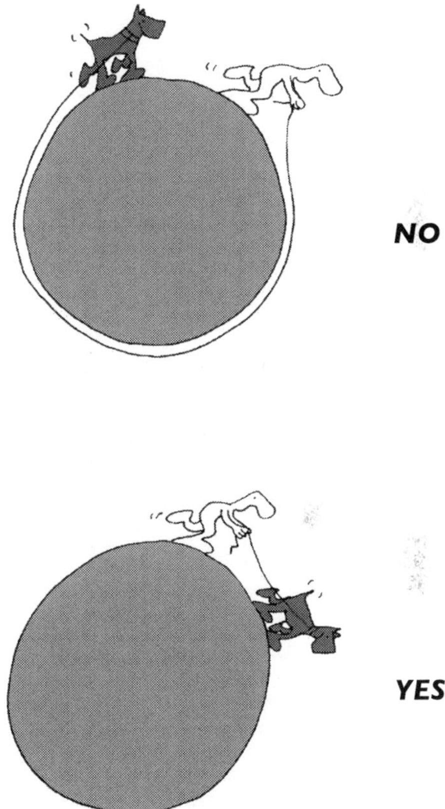

How to *get Toast through a Toast Detector Undetected*

Happiness is having someone
I can talk to about anything...

Appreciate the small things in life

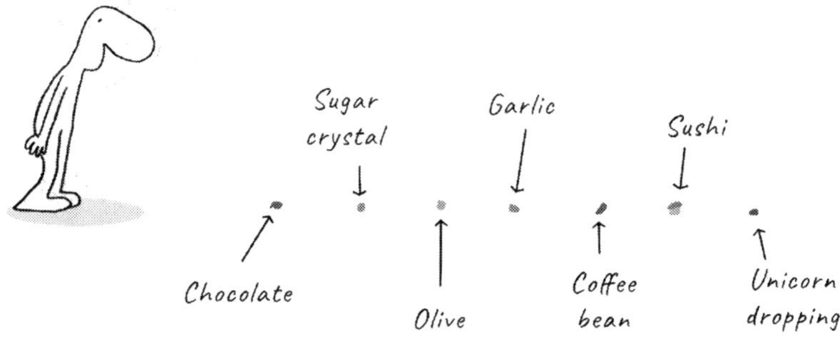

LAWS OF NATURE #17

There's no such thing as ***too much chocolate***

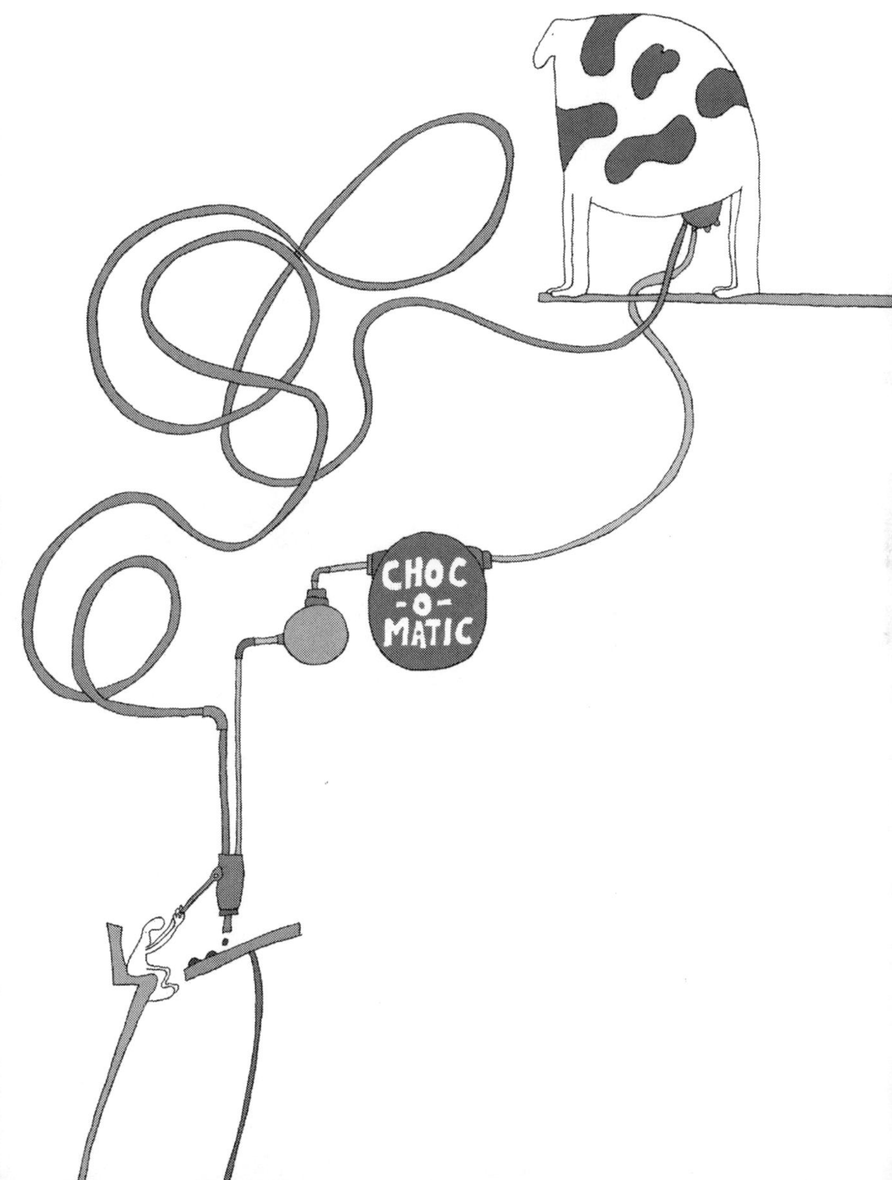

HOW TO *RELAX*

(1) *Plant small stone.*

(2) *Wait patiently as it grows.*

(3) *Almost ready.*

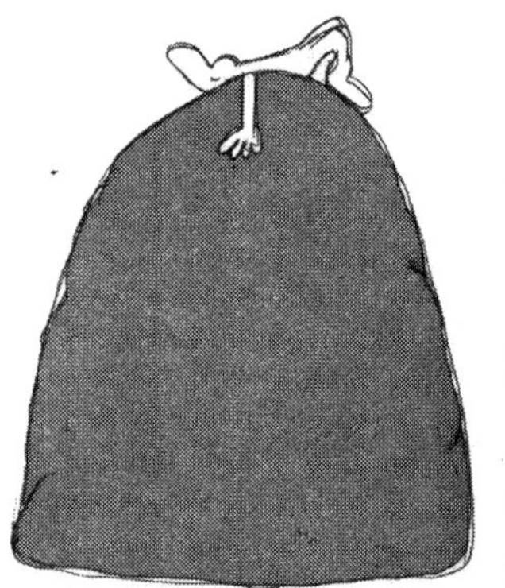

(4) *Lie in sun atop rock. Slowly fall asleep.*

The story of my life...

it's in a book somewhere...

but I can't remember where I put it...

The Perfect Spot

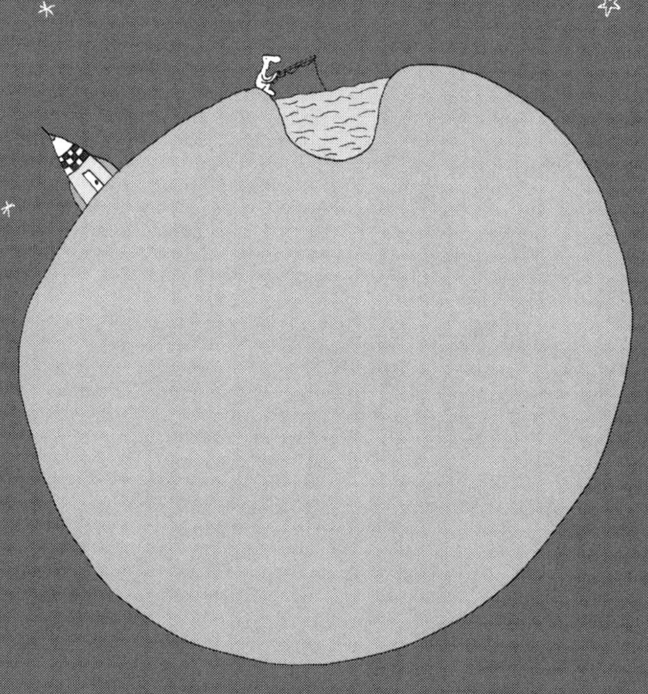

SIMPLE PLEASURES #28

A comfortable silence

Every sunny day I place a chocolate on my head and wait for it to melt. Then I lick it off.

And why do I do this? Because it is the way of my people.

How to Escape from the Woes of the World

① Fill a wheelbarrow with sand

② Walk to the beach

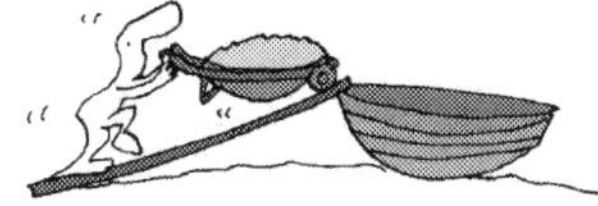

③ Put into rowboat

④ Row out to sea

⑤ Pour into the middle of the ocean

⑥ Row back to beach

⑦ Repeat exercise a few thousand times

⑧ Row back with a small palm tree

⑨ Voila

TICK BOX
YES
NO

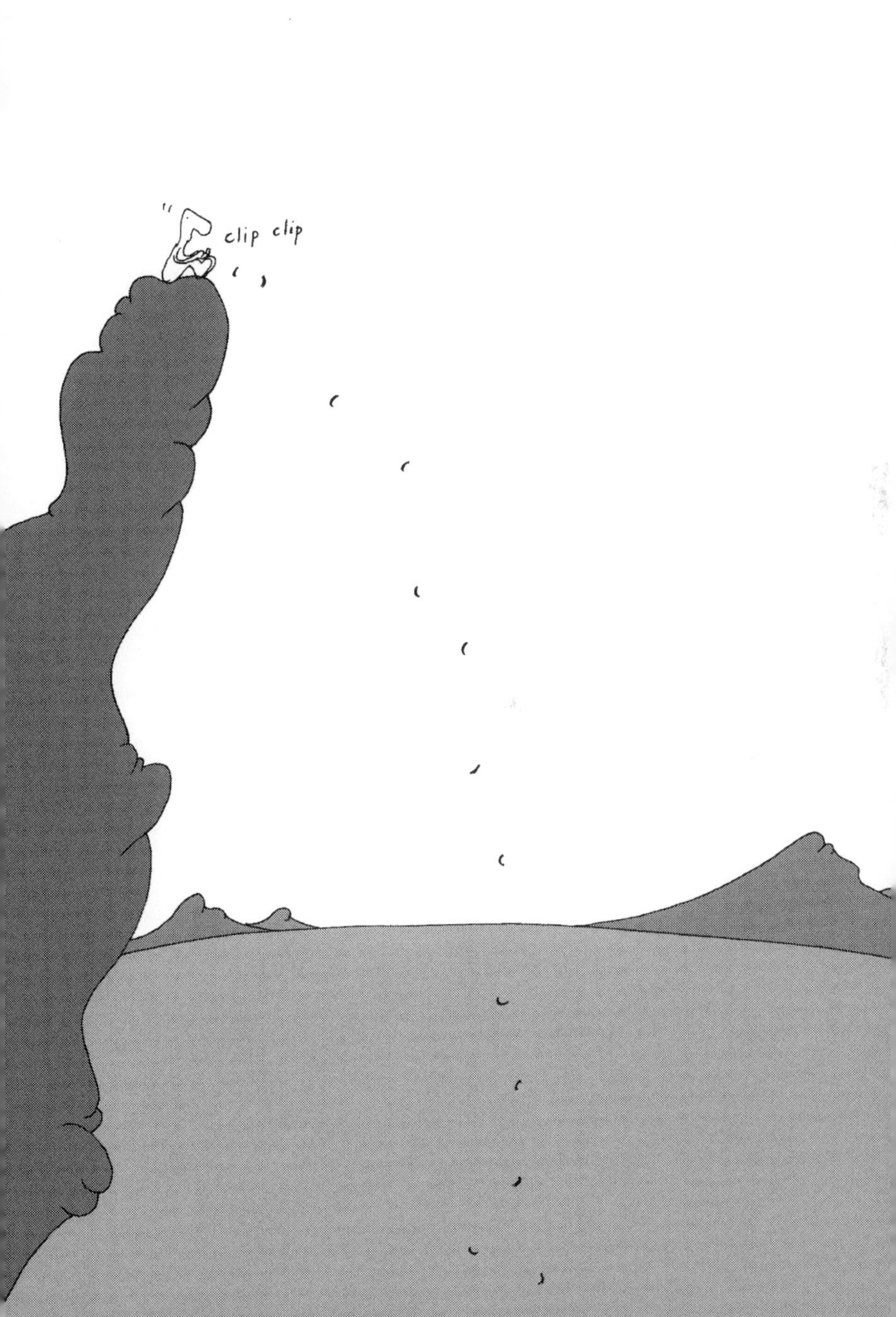
clip clip

How to Escape from an Office

ALWAYS CARRY A SMALL SPADE AND A JAR OF JELLYBEANS.

IF AN OFFICE APPROACHES...

...QUICKLY DIG HOLE.

HIDE IN HOLE.

QUIETLY EAT JELLYBEANS AS OFFICE PASSES OVERHEAD IN SEARCH OF ANOTHER VICTIM.

VOILA.

Sushi lunch

Digital cameras
EXPLAINED

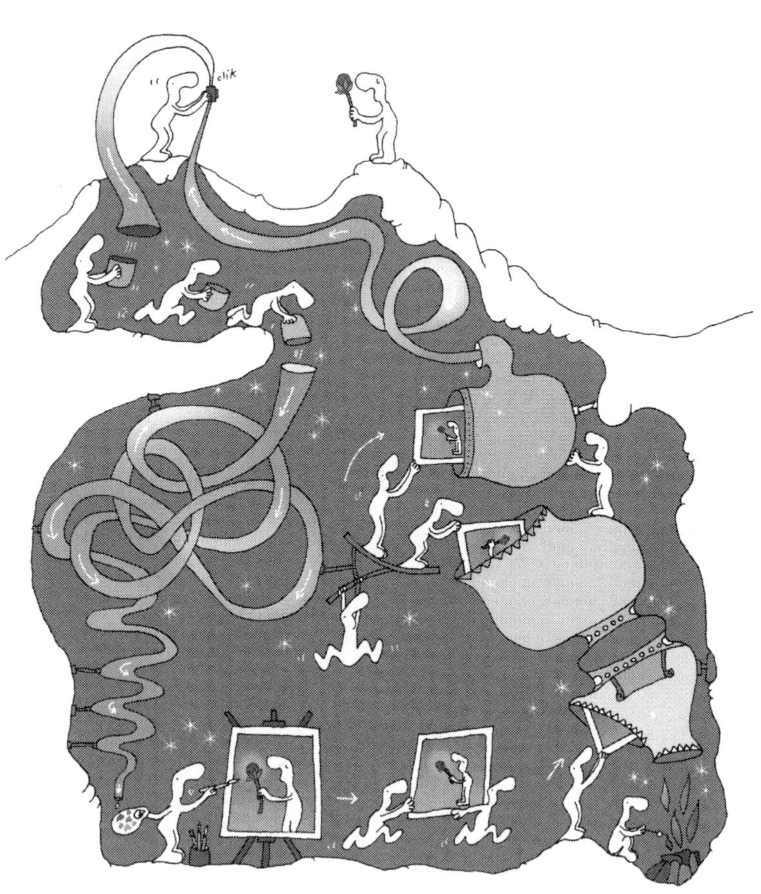

My favourite step

tresspassers
will be
prosecuted

tresspassers
will be
prosecuted

tresspassers
will be
prosecuted

tresspassers
will be
ected

tresspassers
will be

tresspassers
will be
tickled

Stay inspired

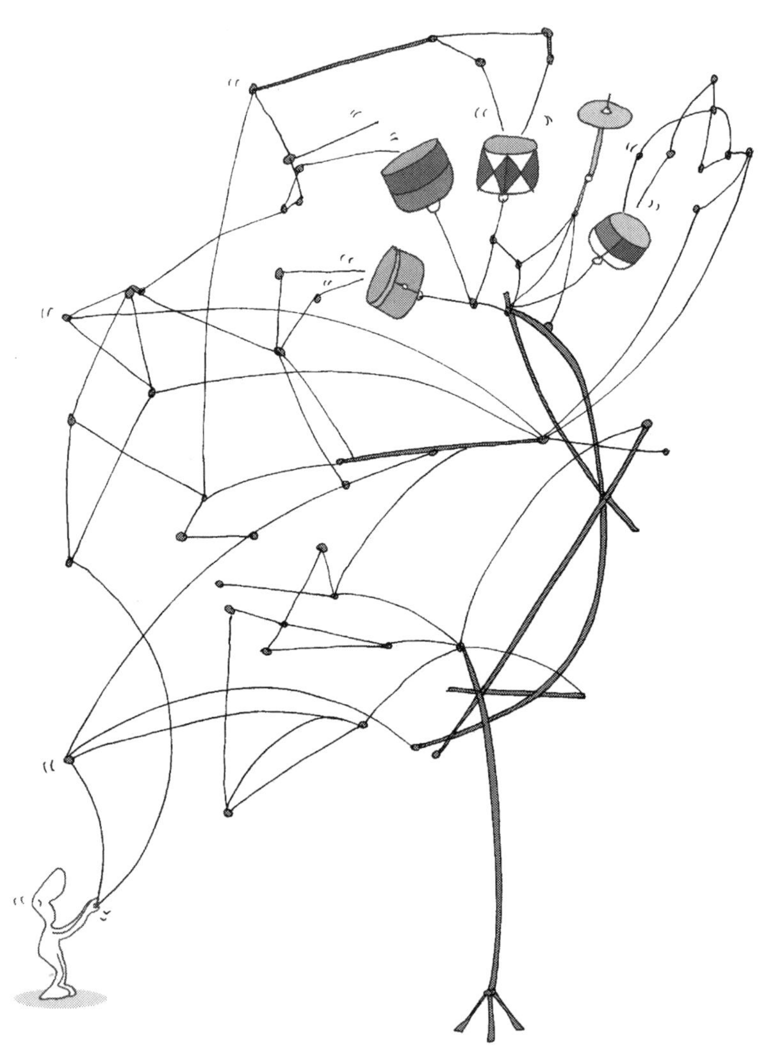

A special friendship

"The softest things in the world overcome the hardest things in the world"

- Lao Tzu -

How to *get ten hours of undisturbed sleep*

GET BUCKET.

FILL WITH WATER.

PUT PHONE IN IT.

PUT ALARM CLOCK IN IT.

GET BED.

GET INTO BED.

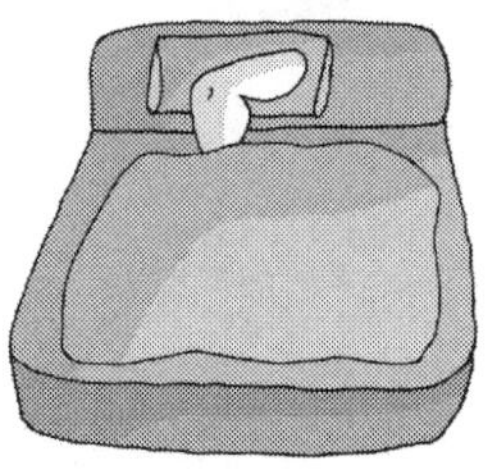

CLOSE EYES AND SLEEP (FOR AT LEAST 10 HOURS.)

TWO RULES FOR SUCCESS

1. Don't tell people everything you know.

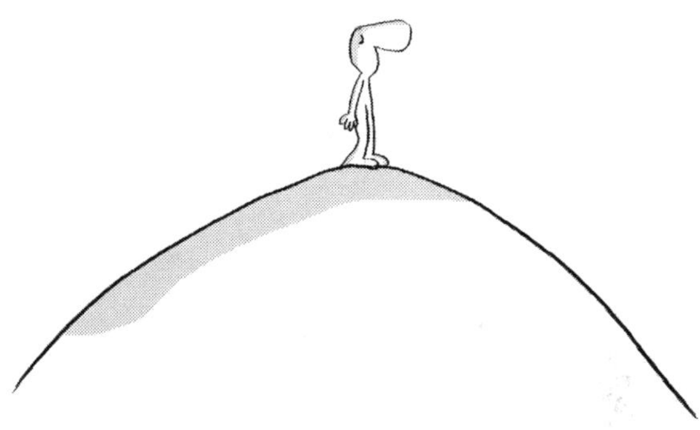

How the Teacup was Invented

The sky smiles on those
who are nice to ants

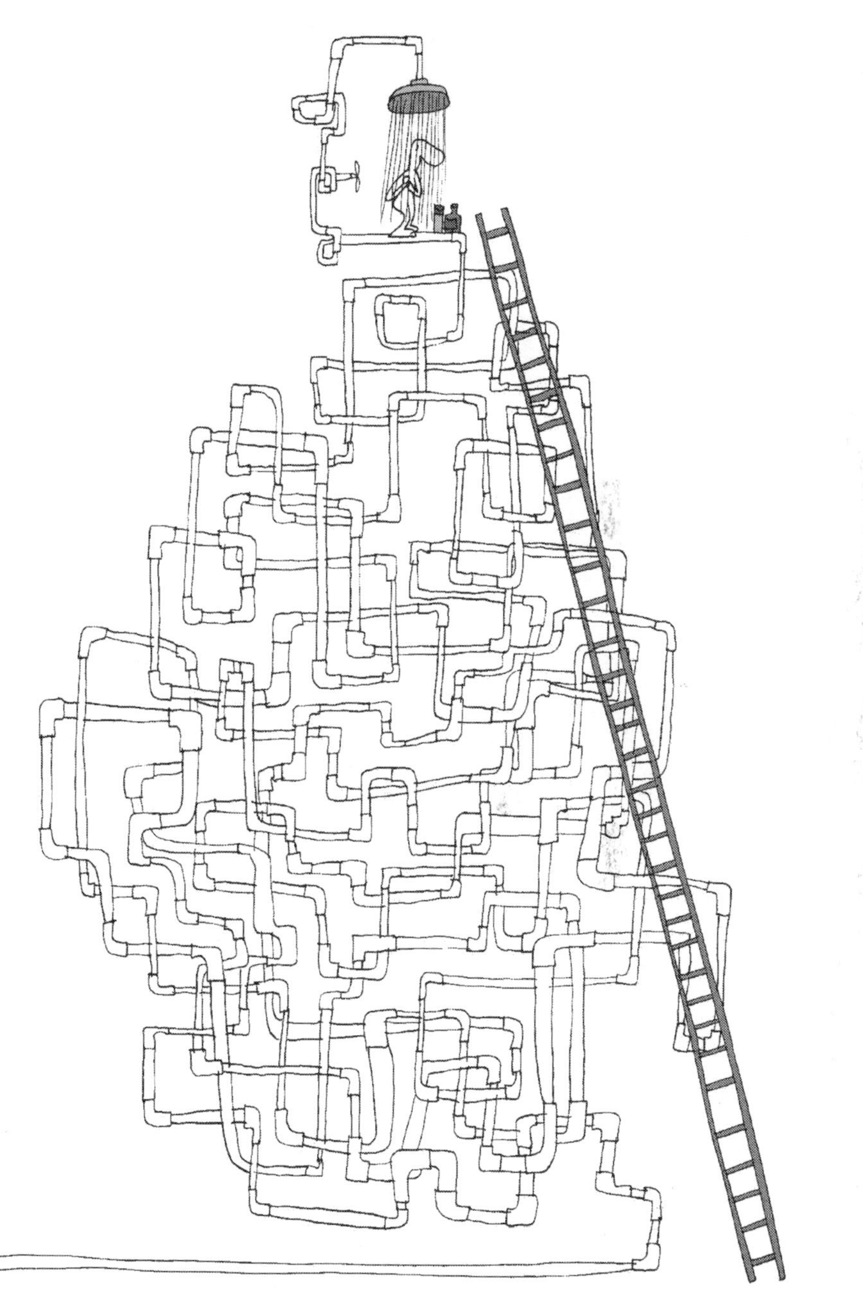

ALL HAIL
The Bath Goddess

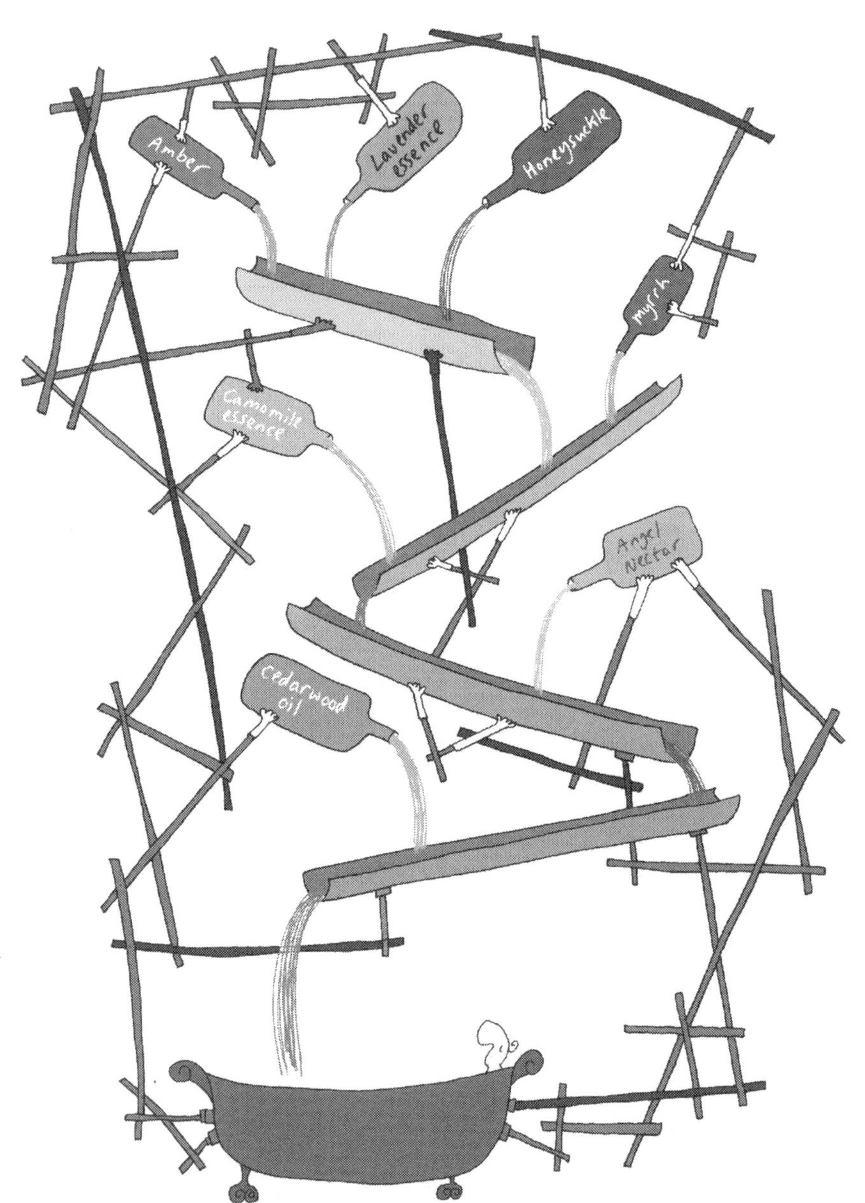

HOW TO *AVOID GETTING STRESSED AT WORK*

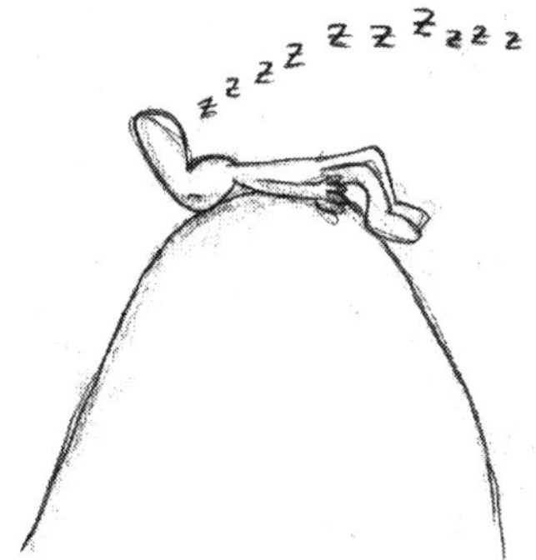

Don't go to work.

Just popping
out for a mo

To sleep or to surf?

That is the question.

LATIN BASICS: LESSON 2

Carpe Diem
(seize the day)

Carpe Noctem
(seize the night)

Carpe Cheesecakeum
(seize the cheesecake)

Don't take life too seriously

HOW TO DEAL WITH TUESDAYS

1. Find a wheelbarrow.
2. Fill it with lovely warm water and bubble bath.
3. Stay there till Wednesday.

The Good Neighbour

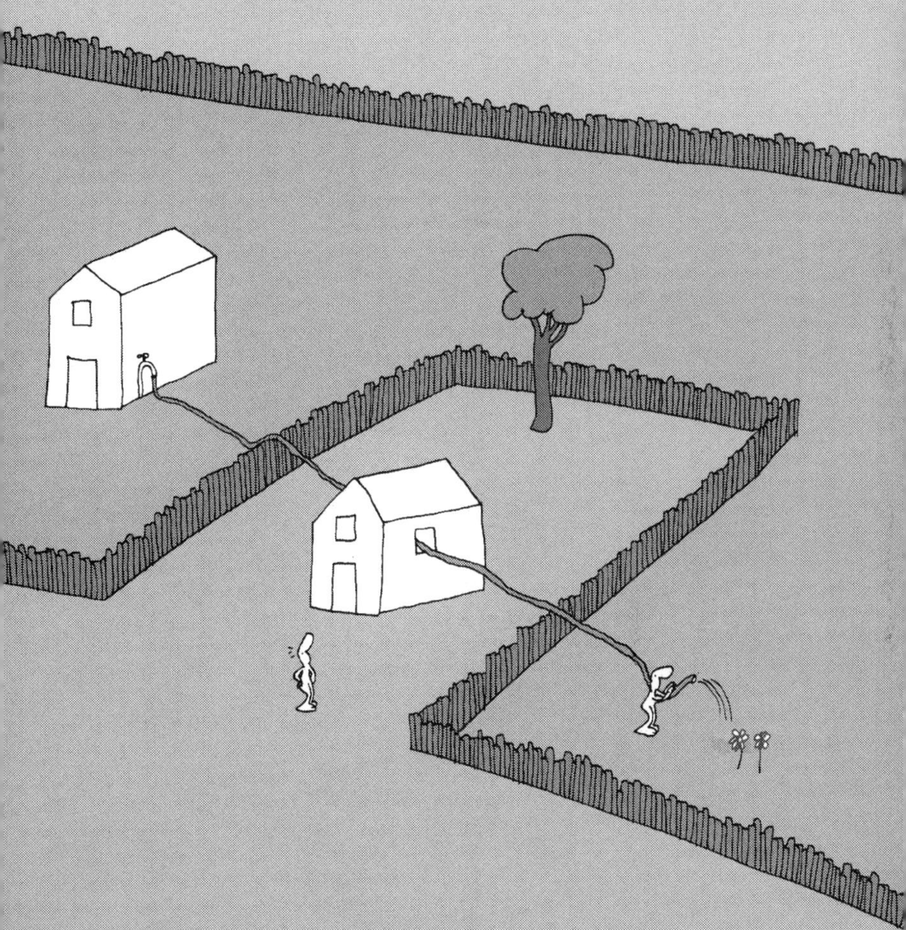

Always take a hug along with you

(you just never know when you might need it)

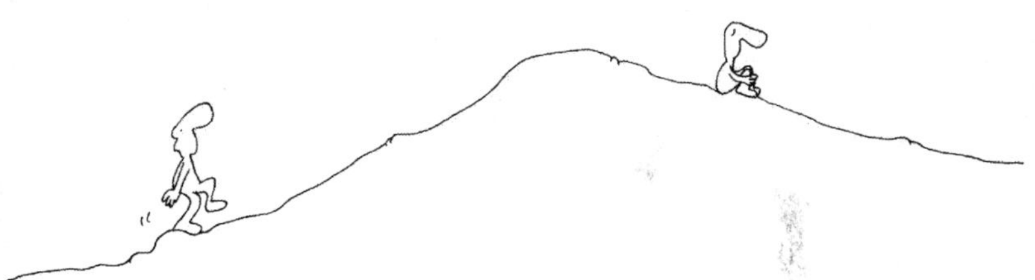

Def: *TYPOPHOBIA*

The fear of speling mistakes

YOGA

for people who don't want to get out of bed

There is no certainty;
but there is adventure...

The avid reader

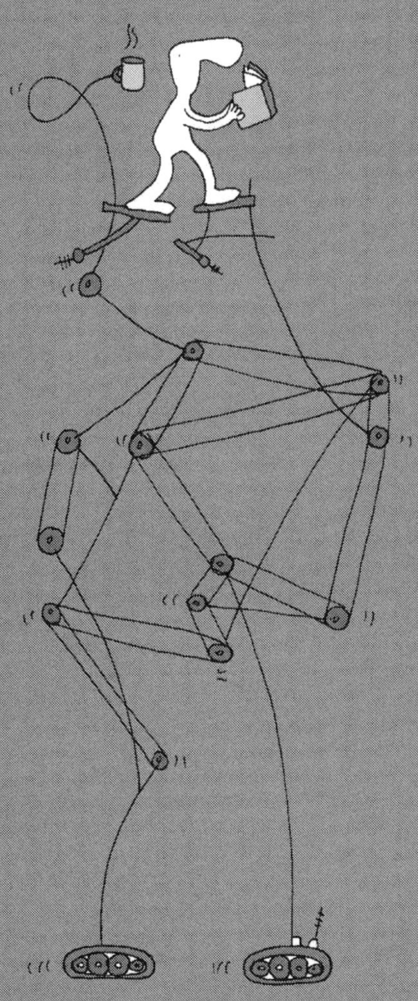

How to *Reduce the Size of your Mobile Phone so you are Sexier*

① *Too large.*

② *Place in toaster.*

③ *Wait patiently.*

④ *Voilå!*

hee hee hoho
hahahaha
haaaaaaaaaa..
LIFE

Tips for Office Survival

1. Avoid all meetings

2. Never offer to make coffee.

3. Avoid all paperwork.

4. Ignore all emails.

5. Try to not annoy anyone.

3. Don't ever answer the phone.

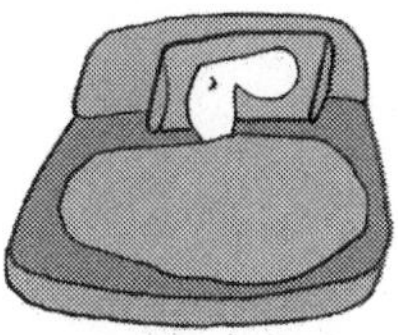

i.e. rather just stay at home, preferably in bed...

Travelling teddy-bear salesmen

THE PIANIST

There's no such thing
as too much yoga...

ONE DAY I WILL BE RICH AND FAMOUS

but for now,
I'll just be me.

Life's a Journey

Live simply

How to *Deal with Someone Annoying*

1. BRING THEM A BUCKET OF CHOCOLATES.

2. POUR CHOCOLATES OUT ON THEIR DESK.

3. PLACE THE BUCKET OVER THEIR HEAD.

4. TAKE THE CHOCOLATES FOR YOURSELF.

It's never too late to try something new...

Anything is possible!

ABOUT THE AUTHORS

Lisa Swerling & Ralph Lazar live in California.

They are the creators of the popular illustrated project ***Happiness Is...****, which has sold nearly half a million books and has over three million followers online.*

They also wrote and illustrated the New York Times bestseller ***Me Without You*** *and two other* **HAROLD'S PLANET** *books* ***Smile*** *and* ***Merlot merlittle****, available on Amazon.*

VISIT HAROLD ONLINE

There is a huge library of Harold's Planet cartoons online at ***www.lastlemon.com/harolds-planet***

facebook.com/itsharoldsplanet
instagram.com/harolds.planet

Made in the USA
Coppell, TX
08 January 2020

14227797R00065